THINK LIKE A WARRIOR

HOW TO SPEED UP YOUR SPORT CAREER IN 30 STEPS

Borys Słuszniak 2020©

Copyright © 2020
All rights reserved. No part of this book may be reproduced by any mechanical, photographic, or electronic process, or in the form of a phonographic recording; nor may it be stored in a retrieval system, transmitted, or otherwise be copied for public or private use — other than for 'fair use' as brief quotations embodied in articles and reviews — without prior written permission of the publisher/author.

LIST OF METHODS:

1. Find The Reason For Practicing A Sport 4
2. Listen To Your Inner Voice 6
3. Set Your Goals High 7
4. Split Your Dreams Into Smaller Goals.. 9
5. Analyze Your Skills.. 11
6. Put Your Goal List In A Visible Place... 14
7. Think About Things That You Have Under Control 15
8. Practice Meditation 17
9. Visualize The Situation 19
10. Set Your Mindset To Personal Growth.. 21
11. Notice The Randomness Of Your Own Beliefs 23
12. Copy The Behavior Of The Best People... 26
13. Relax Your Muscles 28
14. Train Consciously 29
15. Adopt Self-Control.. 33
16. Be Optimistic 35
17. Enter The Flow State... 41
18. Create A Supportive Environment 43
19. Train With People That Are Better Than You 45
20. Reject The Talent Myth.. 47
21. Trust In Yourself.. 51
22. Create Your Pre-Start Routine... 52
23. Don't Listen To Haters.. 54
24. Start To Love Stress 55
25. Practice Selective Attention 57
26. Train More Often Than Others... 60
27. Do Not Forget About Motor Training... 64
28. Be In Charge Of What You Eat... 66
29. Analyze Your Game 68
30. Regenerate Your Body And Mind... 70

Summary 72

1. FIND THE REASON FOR PRACTICING A SPORT

"You wouldn't have won if we'd beaten you."
Yogi Berra

Studies carried out on athletes from all over the world clearly show, that the highest achieved success rate is by people who exactly understand their needs, and most of all they can clearly answer the question:
WHY THEY train?

Are there moments in your life, when you don't want to train or your coach is not satisfied with your results?

Every athlete experienced that situation, but only the best of the best can reverse that feeling and get back on the right track.
Have you ever wondered how they manage to do this?

Here is the answer:
When they feel a lack of energy for training, they remind themselves of the reasons why they started practicing sport in the first place.

Here I collected quotes of famous athletes from different sport disciplines:

-"I give all I have got because I want to be the best goalkeeper in the history of my country"

-"I train because I want to go to the Olympicsand win the gold vmedal"

-"When I didn't feel like training, I visualize myself standing on an Olympic podium."

-"When I had no motivation to wake up at 4 in the morning, I thought about the promise I made to my mother just before her death"

-"I train harder than other people because I want to prove to myself and to others, that a simple boy from the countryside can make his dreams come true".

-"There was no need to give me more motivation. Late evening, when I was coming back home from training, I saw how my friends are on a downward spiral. I didn't want to end up like them, and sport was my only way to escape from this bad path."

-,,Success is not about never falling down, but to stand up every time you fail."

When you have a really strong reason for **WHY** you are training then you will always have answer for the question of **HOW**.

2. LISTEN TO YOUR INNER VOICE

"Adversity causes some men to break; others to break records."
William Arthur Ward

**The subconscious process in our brain is suggesting
our conscious-ness which decisions will agree with our beliefs.
Most people trivialize this fact and make decisions based on their
so-called common sense. The history of high-value individuals
shows, that following your intuition, which is that silent voice
coming "deep from your heart", is the right method
for a satisfactory and fulfilled life.**

Each one of us is predisposed to do something unique.
Our purpose in life should be finding something, that we can devote ourselves entirely to it.

We should not rely on the opinion of other people when it comes
to our talents and things that we are able to accomplish. If you feel
that your purpose in life is to be a top-class athlete, then make
a conscious decision to walk this path and never have any doubts
about your choice.
Right now, you may feel that it could hard to be real, but after
a few years, when you look back, your perspective will dramatically
change. You will see that everything will fall into place.

*"You can't connect the dots looking forward; you can only connect
them looking backwards. So you have to trust that the dots
will somehow connect in your future. You have to trust
in something - your gut, destiny, life, karma, whatever.
This approach has never let me down, and it has made all
the difference in my life." – Steve Jobs*

3. SET YOUR GOALS HIGH

"The five S's of sports training are: stamina, speed, strength, skill, and spirit; but the greatest of these is spirit." Ken Doherty

It is very hard to have a steadfast motivation that is on the verge of an obsession when our dreams are not ambitious. Biographies of Olympic Champions clearly show, that their adventure with sport began from setting a big goal in which they truly believed they will achieve.

Everyone should have something in their life, that is worth the sacrifice. It is hard to do that when your dreams are not kindling your imagination. In order to achieve great things, you have to "soak up" with it to the point, where you don't have any doubt that you can fulfill your dream. You have to constantly think about it, see it in front of you and speak openly. Only then you will be ready for real physical effort. A lot of athletes are scared of brave decisions. They are afraid of being laughed at by other less ambitious colleagues. They content themselves with a "realistic" view of the world. They lack self-confidence. They adjust to the mediocre, ordinary people.

You need to remember this. **In order to achieve success, you have to become "abnormal".** You have to think differently. Be ambitious and brave.

When you create various life plans (in case it did not work out in sports), you automatically assume that you are acting reasonably and securing your future. Unfortunately, when you have a plan B, it is more like that you will back out. You will not bite the bullet like people who put all the eggs in one basket.

Being realistic is perfectly normal, but don't delude yourself that with such an attitude you will achieve greatness.

> *"Impossible is just a big word thrown around by small men who find it easier to live in the world they've been given than to explore the power they have to change it. Impossible is not a fact. It's an opinion. Impossible is not a declaration. It's a dare. Impossible is potential. Impossible is temporary. Impossible is nothing."* Muhammad Ali

4. SPLIT YOUR DREAMS INTO SMALLER GOALS

"Persistence can change failure into extraordinary achievement." Marv Levy

When you compare athletic career to driving a car: When your route is the longer, more complicated and less known, the more important it is to have a map or GPS navigation that will guide you to move towards the right direction.

During a trip, it is not all about driving a car (despite what many people consider this a lot of fun), but it is about relocating from point A to point B. Even if you chose a wrong turn, you will still move, unfortunately not in the right direction. You will be on tour, but you will never reach the goal.

It is very similar to your sports dreams. You have to split them into smaller goals, such as targets that are annual, monthly, weekly and daily. That way you will be sure what,
how and where to do things.

Thanks to well-written map (I should emphasize this - well written, not well though), you will avoid feeling discouraged, due to the long distance to your main goal (dream) and you will know about forthcoming tasks in the near future.

An example of intermediate objectives set by a football player:

Playing the game next year in the league one is an ambitious task for a player, but realistic. If he will train hard and for a long time, then his skill level will rise to such an extent, that he will be ready to play the game on a major-league level. Finally, when he will reach one step above, his perspective will change. The next goal – to play in Champion League becomes more realistic than one year or even two years before.

> *"I always felt that my greatest asset was not my physical ability, it was my mental ability."*
> *Bruce Jenner*

5. ANALYZE YOUR SKILLS

"Continuous effort - not strength or intelligence - is the key to unlocking our potential."
Liane Carde

The main key to self-development is awareness of your own weaknesses and strengths. A lot of athletes make this mistake they focus only on exercises that they are good at. As the old saying goes:

"You are as strong, as your weakest link".

Every sport discipline can be broken down into individual elements, and to every element, you can assign any skill, that accounts for its quality.

For example, if you are a football player, one of the key elements is speed, where quality accounts for such skills as response time, speeding up on a short length, running technique, right movement of hands, etc.

The best athletes from all over the world differ in their disciplines with small nuances. Only when there is properly diagnosed poorly developed skill, they are able to prepare their training to make constant progress.

It is important for you to realize your strengths and weaknesses in order to create your own skill profile.

Instruction on how to create your profile:

"You are as strong, as your weakest link"

1. Write down 8 elements, that are the most important in your discipline
2. In every area rate yourself on a scale of 1 to 10 and mark it ona chart
3. Choose 3 elements, where you gave yourself the lowest score
4. Focus more time on that area till you reach the same point as in other areas or even exceed them

1 2 3 4 5 6 7 8 9 10

Profile example of a football player:

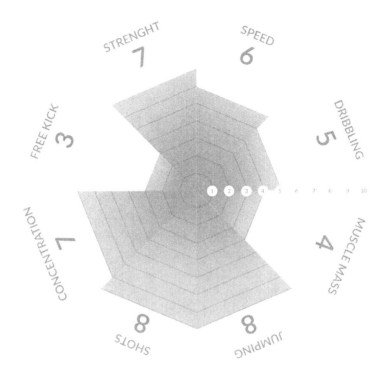

By creating this profile, the player benefited a key element for the development of every athlete - **awareness**.
When creating a profile, I always use its analogy to a car wheel. I suggest visualizing, that a wheel from your car has the same shape as your profile. Your goal is to fill that empty space in your wheel, in order to make your trip safe. That way athletes start to understand, that their work should start from these areas, which have the biggest "empty space". In the case of a football player, that "empty space" is muscle mass, dribbling, and free-kick technique. Those are the things that he should focus on in the near future.

> *"The principle is competing against yourself.*
> *It's about self-improvement, about being better than*
> *you werethe day before."*
> *Steve Young*

6. PUT YOUR GOAL LIST IN A VISIBLE PLACE

"You are never really playing an opponent. You are playing yourself, your own highest standards, and when you reach your limits, that is real joy."
Arthur Ashe

Every person that unsuccessfully tried to persevere in the resolution knows, that there comes a moment when we believe that we can let go just this once. We are not aware that the old habit has the advantage over the new one just the same as a rally driver over the person, who just started to learn how to drive.

Skills of a rally driver are so developed, that even if he missed driving for 10 years, thanks to such extended practice and experience, will drive much better than a rookie driver. It works that way because his brain has ready mental patterns, which require only a quick "dusting off" his skills. When you are a rookie, everything is in the phase of creation. The same rule applies to resolutions.
If you are not trying to completely get rid of your old habits, and you do it only once then there is a high probability that everything will revert to the previous state. This is why it is so important not to forget about your goals, put them in such a place where you look every day. For example, it can be a mirror in the bathroom, wall in a room, on a desk, wallpaper in your smartphone or computer.
It is essential that you additionally write a date of implementation to avoid the temptation of postponing.

"It ain't about how hard you can hit. It's about how hard you can get hit, and keep moving forward."
Sylvester Stallone, Rocky Balboa

7. THINK ABOUT THINGS THAT YOU HAVE UNDER CONTROL

"The mind is the limit. As long as the mind can envision the fact that you can do something, you can do it, as long as you really believe 100 percent." Arnold Schwarzenegger

The most often situations that upset us are the ones which we cannot in control in any way: judges, coach, opponent, fans or even bad weather. When you learn to concentrate only on those elements that you can control, you will greatly benefit in the quality of your performance.

Analyze your training and matches from the perspective, where they adversely affect your game and ask yourself if they were out of your control. If not, then write them down on a piece of paper and name it „Beyond my control"

On the other side of the note write specific situations, which had a negative impact on your game, but you were unable to avoid them. Only those, that were in the scope of your control. They can be classified as one of those 5 categories:

- your **thoughts**, f.e. „I am unable to do this"
- your **emotions**, f.e. Frustration
- your **body posture** f.e avoiding eye-contact
- your **effort** f.e. Reduction in involvement during the match
- your **decisions** f.c. You miss one training, because „I don't really feel like it"

It is important for you to realize, **that the situations are not responsible for spoiling your game, it is you and the way you react to them.** Let's analyze specific situation during the game and their potential effects:

1. (**THOUGHTS**) „He took my score again, and because of that I may lose"
2. (**EMOTIONS**) There is frustration, self-doubt.
3. (**BODY POSTURE**) Your body becomes tense, you start to make nervous movements.
4. (**EFFORT**) Your commitment and concentration are reduced because energy is dissipated in other directions.
5. (**DECISION**) You start to think about what will happen next and you look for the reasons for the failure "if I lose it is judge's fault." You are starting to give up.

It is important to perceive the cause and effect relationship between what you say to yourself, and how you feel and behave during your performance or training.

Maybe you only need to see one destructive thought and change it into something positive, like:

> *„Fight till the end like a lion". That way maybe you will change the quality of your performance?"*

The situations that you encounter are not responsible for your fate, it is you and the way you react to them.

8. PRACTICE MEDITATION

"If you can believe it, the mind can achieve it."
Ronnie Lott

Despite the fact, that the term „meditation" is commonly known, most people don't understand what it means and how easy it is to use. A lot of professional athletes meditate, and a lot of players in sports teams like Chicago Bulls or Borussia Dortmund have their own meditation coaches.

Meditation is a way to clear your head and is based on concentration on your own breath and other senses that occur in your body.
It is a great way to deal with stress and negative thoughts.

Athletes exactly know that feeling, when pushy thoughts and uncontrolled emotions ruin their months of training.

Meditating for 15 minutes will after few weeks give real benefits and will solve problems mentioned previously. A lot of medical studies confirm that.

So, don't wait and including this technique in your training routine.

Instruction for a simple meditation:

Find a quiet place, where you can be completely alone with yourself. Sit on a chair or lie on your back. Find yourself a comfortable position. Close your eyes and concentrate on your breath.

Do not change anything. Just be yourself. Focus on how you inhale and exhale the air. Don't expect anything, just concentrate on your breath. When you do it properly, you will feel a moment of a clear mind.

After a few breaths, you will feel that thoughts are intrinsically filling your mind without your control. Observe this phenomenon and focus again on your breath. Remember to do it gently and without any judgment. Let yourself be the person you are right now in this specific moment and slowly watch your body and mind. Enjoy the gentle feeling of a silent mind.

„My emotional downfalls are most often very flat because everything depends on the way I think or the way I try to think for most of the time. Psychologists name this state „mindfulness training" and its main goal is to clear your mind and find your inner peace. The main trick is to observe your thoughts objectively, without any judgment, focusing your attention on this right moment in real-time. The important part of this exercise is to be quiet and focused. If you do this on a regular basis, even for a short amount of time, you will learn a lot of new things about yourself, because you will learn to perceive the current moment."
Novak Djoković

9. VISUALIZE THE SITUATION

"To uncover your true potential you must first find your own limits and then you have to have the courage to blow past them."
Picabo Street

It has been proven, that if you visualize specifically trained activities, you will trigger the same area of the brain that is used during the real activity. This shows that visualization can be an effective way of improving your skills and preparing for sports competition.

If you properly perform the visualization, it will help you create a kind of mirror reflection of your sports skills. It's effectiveness depends on how vivid (and real) are scenes in your imagination.
The more senses you will use, the better.

See, feel and hear all the possible elements of the recreated image. Place your images in the competition scenery and if possible,
look at everything from your own perspective.

When you lack motivation, visualize yourself achieving great success. Imagine how good it feels. Believe, that if you can imagine it then you can achieve it. I am sure that you know yourself very well and you are familiar with your sport discipline, so you can foresee different situations during the competition f.e. stress before the beginning, lack of self-confidence after making some mistakes, decrease
of concentration because of fan whistling during your performance.

Write them down and spend each day a few minutes recreating this image, where you manage to cope with them very well. Thanks to this, no matter what happens, you will be very well-prepared for them.

How to get involved in each and every sense of the visualization?
Example: receiving a strong ball serve during a volleyball match

- **Sight** - you see the ball being thrown up in the air, the moment when it gets hit, the trajectory of the ball, and next how your body and hands are positioned. You see how the ball bounces perfectlyon your hands – just the way you wanted it to bounce – and next with an optimal trajectory flies to the quarterback near the net.
- **Hearing** – you hear the moment when the ball is hit by the opponent, you hear a voice in your head shouting „it is mine!", and next you hear a characteristic sound of the ball being hit by your forearms.
- **Smell** – you smell the sports hall, ball, and your team shirt.
- **Touch** – you can feel that you firmly stand on your feet, how you balance the weight of your body when you put your forearms to receive the ball, you feel how the ball hits the forearms, how you amor-tize the impact. Try to feel the energy which your body receives during the moment of bouncing the ball.
- **Emotions** – feel the involvement when hitting the ball. Feel how well you are concentrated. Right now, nothing else matters to you. Feel positive self-confidence.

How to choose the skill to visualize?

1. **Choose the 5 most important technical elements in your sport discipline.** For example in footballer: long passes, dribbling, shot from behind the penalty area, slides.

2. **Choose 3 elements that in your opinion should be improved.** Remember and make sure that you visualize the right technique. Visualize perfectly performed three of the above elements for 15 minutes per day.

"Excellence is the gradual result of always striving to do better."
Pat Riley

10. SET YOUR MINDSET TO PERSONAL GROWTH

*"I performed many visualizations before Olympic qualifying rounds.
I think it helped me feel how it would look when I get there."*
Michael Phelps.

**American psychologist Carl Dweck found out, that success is determined by the way you see your own skills. Thanks to this discovery we know that people can be divided into two categories: people focused on sustainability or on self-development.
Check to which group you belong to.**

Studies have shown that athletes have different ways of perceiving their own potential. People that are focused on sustainability believe, that their attributes are set in stone. On the other hand, people focused on self-development belief, that they can constantly develop thanks to hard work.

The consequence of such belief is as follows: when the first-mentioned group has to constantly prove their own value and avoids any challenges not to undermine their own ego, the second group tries to break their boundaries, and **they treat effort and defeat as a thing that is necessary for self-development**. Athletes that aim to development never give up expanding their horizons, because **they treat their own potential as something infinite**. Conviction and hard work are the main keys to achieving fantastic results.

Spend the next few days focusing on your own way of thinking.
Rate how they influence your attitude during the training.
Pay close attention to how you see your own success and the success of other people. Do you assume that it can be achieved thanks to hard work or talent?

Analyze what you think about your own failures. Are they a valuable lesson and their main goal is to improve your skills? Do they indicate that you have limited abilities and you cannot do anything with that?

I have prepared an infographic for you, which shows 8 main areas that are important from the motivational point of view of hard work during training. They result from the type of your own attitude. It is very probable that you have a combination of both attitudes.

If that is true, appreciate and emphasize even more everyday areas that are aimed towards development. As far as those regarding attitude, try to make them permanent.

> *"You need to have dreams, you need to go for it, otherwise why would you be a footballer?"*
> *Virgil van Dijk*

11. NOTICE THE RANDOMNESS OF YOUR OWN BELIEFS

"Some people think football [soccer] is a matter of life and death. I don't like that attitude. I can assure them it is much more serious than that."
Bill Shankly

We come into the world with a certain set of genes inherited after our ancestors. Consequently, many people assume, that we don't have much influence on whom we really become. It turns out that life success is determined by behaviors, beliefs, and attitudes that we learn from other people.

When we come to this world, we are like a clear, blank page. **You are not born with an idea about yourself.** We are not even conscious that we are a separate being.

More or less around 18 months of our lives, we realize that „you" is not the same as your mother or father. At this point, you are able to distinguish yourself from others. You don't have any influence on who you are becoming, what is happening to you and how you are raised. Your parents are taking care of „creating you" during the next few years. You start to live according to their idea.

When you are around 5 years old, you start to have the first inner dialogues. You start to live according to what your brain tells you, and **your mind is shaped by the reality that you were located.** Personality is being created, which is based on raising by your parents and the environment that you are living in.

This is the stage of life when for the first-time ego appears, created due to the effect of current experience.

The behavior of a small child becomes a mirror reflection of his parents. It does not know the world or the reality that he is living in, and that is why it is learning on the basis of own observation. You can say that from the early years, you are developed according to a pattern, which was created by the experience of other people.

You start to treat the beliefs that you learn during that period of time as your own and there is a high probability, that you will have them in your heart till you die. It is great if those beliefs are beneficial, worse if they limit your potential.

Look at yourself from the perspective of an observer. Look for a belief in yourself, that you don't like, or you feel like they restrict your potential. Next, perform the exercise presented below.

Check the authenticity of your own beliefs:
Use a method called Rational Behavior Therapy created by M.C. Maultsby. It will help you evaluate if a specific belief is "healthy" and rational. If you have a belief that is doubtful, use these 5 questions. If you answer negatively on at least 3 of them, then the belief is unhealthy and you should change it.

1. Is this belief based on facts?
2. Does it save life or health?
3. Does it help to reach close or long-term goals?
4. 4. Does it help to resolve conflicts or avoid them in the first place?
5. Does it let me feel just the way I want?

Robert is a football player. This is his example:
Belief: I am too short to play in the Champions League

1. Is it based on facts?
No, because there are many football players even shorter which play in the Champions League.
2. Saves life or health?
Hard to say, but you can for sure notice that it does do any harm.
3. Helps to reach close or long-term goals?
No, you stop believing in your dreams.
4. Helps to resolve conflicts?
I don't know
5. Lets me feel just the way I want?
No, it makes me feel disappointed and it reduces my motivation.

CONCLUSION: 3 answers were **NEGATIVE**, so Robert's beliefs are not healthy and rational. It is false and it has to be changed.

"Becoming a footballer is only the first half of the silent prayer a kid offers up to the sky or confides to his teacher in a primary school essay. The second part is the name of the team he wants to play for."
Andrea Pirlo

12. COPY THE BEHAVIOR OF THE BEST PEOPLE

"You have to fight to reach your dream. You have to sacrifice and work hard for it."
Lionel Messi

The personality of a champion is based on a set of features, which decide about human excellence. While observing the best athletes in the world, you can easily come to the conclusion, that they are born masterminds with supernatural powers. It may appear that they are destined for greatness. But the reality is somehow dif-ferent. It is high time you get familiar with the real facts.

Nowadays in the world, there is a myth in which talent is responsible for fantastic achievements.

Yes, talent may occur, but it does more harm than good, especially for young athletes. When a young person hears that they have this "special gift" there is a high probability, that it will stop working hard. He may think that if he has talent, he does not have to spend so much time on training. After a few years he becomes a „waste of talent".

Having talent is definitely not enough to become the best of the best. Studies clearly show, that best athletes have these characteristics:

- Passion
- Strong work ethics
- Focus on one discipline
- Orderliness
- Desire to broaden own horizons
- Using the feedback

None of the mentioned above features work like some kind of magic potion. What is more, you have an influence on each one of these elements.

Very often athletes have some of those elements, e.g. they have pas-sion, they work hard and want to get better and better, but unfortunately, they lack resistance to failure and the ability to focus on things that are most important. Only the full synergy of all the features can create the foundation of the outstanding athletes.

Even just the awareness of the fact that there is such a thing as a masterful personality should give you faith in your own abilities. Your idols were once in the same place as you are right now, and very often even in a worse place. However, they understood what to follow in life in order to achieve success.

They made a decision.
It is up to you! You can also make a decision at any given moment.

Find your sports idol. Read his biography, check out his quotes, watch his performances. Look for the features that make him so unique and try to implement them in your life.

> *"When people succeed, it is because of hard work.*
> *Luck has nothing to do with success."*
> *Diego Maradona*

13. RELAX YOUR MUSCLES

*"You can't put a limit on anything. The more you dream,
the farther you get."*
Michael Phelps

Relaxation is, next to visualization and goal setting, the mental technique most often used by Olympic champions. It involves prac-ticing breathing in conjunction with stretching and loosening cer-tain muscle parts and brings real benefits in dealing with stress be-fore the competition.

This technique is called progressive muscle relaxation or Jacobson Relaxing Training Technique. To perform it, you need sound waves that will take you into a state of deep relaxation. Your task will be to turn on sound waves (read on Wikipedia which sound waves are the best for relaxing or to make your dreams come true, a dark room and a quiet place so that nobody and nothing will distract you during the whole process of muscle relaxation).

Lie down comfortably, close your eyes and with every breath flex each muscle. After the whole process, you'll see the amazing effect of relaxing your muscles. **You will feel calm and regenerated.** This is a very similar method for meditation. Let's get going!

14. TRAIN CONSCIOUSLY

"Some people say I have attitude – maybe I do…but I think you have to. You have to believe in yourself when no one else does – that makes you a winner right there."
Venus Williams

The biggest problem with athletes is that at some stage they stop to develop. Why does this happen? Probably because they are not familiar with the different phases of acquiring new skills.

Athletes often expect that this process will take place in a linearly, i.e.

According to this assumption, with each subsequent training, I will feel how my skills grow.

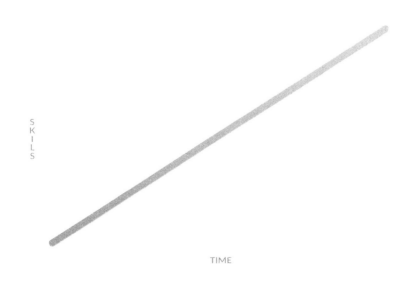

FALSE

This idea of becoming a champion is the most common reason for giving up your sports activity because you start to think that the training is not giving any results.

George Leonard, an American psychologist described in his book "Mastery" how actually looks acquiring new skills.

His studies show that changes in our skills occur abruptly, with elements of growth, plateaus and declines, namely:

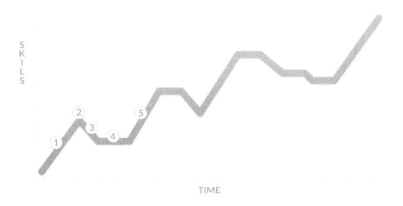

This abruption and basically lack of knowledge about it, is one of the biggest problems that athletes have during maintaining motivation for hard training.
As you can see in the chart, the problem appears at the very first stage: **we train, time passes, and we don't see the expected skills.**

At this moment a lot of people simply give up. If there are no effects, that means I am not suitable and I will give up.

Some people are lucky that when they start their adventure with a given discipline, the **GROWTH** appears immediately (No. 1 on the chart). However, regardless of how your beginning will look like, it is certain that the **PEAK** phase (No. 2) will eventually come, which rapidly goes into the **DECLINE** phase (No. 3).

At this point, it is very important to be aware that the **DECLINE** phase applies only to the peak point and is most often caused by the addition of another new element of learning a given skill.
For example, you are a football player and you want free kicks to become your master's skill. At some point, you will find that an accurate shot in the goal window from 20 meters is not difficult for you. You will soon do it naturally, without much mental effort. Thus, you add another element - wall with five football players.
In this way, you load your mind with a new task that requires maximum focus, new attempts, and ongoing adjustments in the way you shoot.

This task can be in every respect frustrating and exhausting, but it is only an introduction to the worst phase so-called **PLATEAUS** (No. 4). This is a period when you cannot see the effects of your work for a long time. What is more, you still remember the time of great growth and you start to wonder what happened to this player from the previous month. During this period, you are most susceptible to a decrease in training involvement (*"Why should I try to train, if there aren't any effects"*) and a decrease in confidence (*"Unfortunately I'm not as good as I thought"*).

In fact, the plateau is not a period when nothing happens, quite the opposite. During this period, skills are integrated at a deeper level of your brain. Things that you are doing consciously and in full concentration are now being automated, and soon your body will be doing them without your participation.

Therein lie the mastering and the famous state of "flow". Things happen by themselves, and your integrated skills flow out from you.

Your persistent, hard work will soon result in another phase of **GROWTH** (No. 5) and the whole cycle will repeat.
During your sports career, try to find moments that you could match to the stages of acquiring skills, such as unexpectedly great performances or periods of prolonged stagnation.
Then think about whether you recently had or stopped learning one of the elements because you haven't seen the effects of your work. Perhaps you are in the plateau period and it is worth holding tight to your training?
When you know your training is well-designed, be patient. Integrating some skills takes more time than you think.

"There are only two options regarding commitment. You're either IN or you're OUT. There is no such thing as life in-between."
Pat Riley

15. ADOPT SELF-CONTROL

"The highest compliment that you can pay me is to say that I work hard every day, that I never do it."
Wayne Gretzky

American psychologist Walter Mitschel, thanks to his 40 years of research has permanently changed the way of looking at the reasons for succumbing to temptation. When examining young children (few years old), he noticed that those "beings" widely regarded as impulsive and helpless, were able to resist from eating a delicious treat (even when someone promised them to later give them a twice as big reward), by using specific strategies of action.

Those that succeeded did better later in life. Thanks to Mitschel's research, we can use these strategies on a daily basis.

The first major conclusion from his research is that self-control is not something innate and that we can learn it. **In the life of an athlete, there are situations where it is easy to succumb to immediate pleas-ures,** e.g. going to a party, drinking alcohol or eat something unhealthy without thinking about the consequences.
What should we do in such situations?

Well, we should **"chill" the present moment and "heat" the future pleasure, as a result of the fact of resisting the temptation,** e.g. by visualizing your own ideal figure or imagining winning in sports competition. In a situation when we have doubts, we will have a broader perspective. We shall see the relationship between current action and its consequence in the near future.

For this to happen, you must have a previously prepared strategy.
Write a list of "triggering" situations and your desired response. Construct the formula as follows:

IF .... (triggering situation) ...... **THEN** ...... (desired response).
e.g. **IF** I feel like eating sweets, **THEN** I will start to visualize my perfect figure, that way I will change my mind and eat something healthy.
This technique seems trivial, but it is very effective and well known in the psychology of motivation. It's called intentional implementation and is used to program intentional action.

The more you repeat this, the faster it will become a habit that will not require any conscious effort.

It is also worth using the strategy of initial commitments, e.g. If you know that it would be hard for you to train in the morning, simply pack your bag before going to bed, prepare clothes that you will wear tomorrow and put in one place products that you will use to make breakfast, etc. Thanks to that you will take the first step to implement the planned actions and you will drastically increase your chances of waking up on time.

Also, **step back a little from what you do.** When you find it difficult to resist the temptation and you are always looking for justifications of your behavior, try to look at yourself from the perspective of a camera (or as Mitschel said – the perspective of a fly on the wall). The camera does not add any theory or justifications, it only sees what is in front of her. Submission to temptation is exactly what it registers, i.e. acting against its own goals. Adopting an observer's perspective will help you see those moments when you are trying to deceive yourself.

16. BE OPTIMISTIC

"Gold medals aren't really made of gold. They're made of sweat, determination, and a hard-to-find alloy called guts."
Dan Gable

DIFFICULTY – a situation that requires solution
CONVICTION – the standard of conduct
EFFECT
Reaction

One of the greatest discoveries of psychology is the fact that to a great extent, we can choose our way of thinking, particularly how we interpret successful situations and failures (research by Martin Seligman). Pessimistic athletes, in the face of failure, become helpless and perceive failure as something permanent and personal, however athletes that are optimistic distance themselves and treat failure as a lesson that will help them in the future.

For pessimists, the unfavorable experiences of the past create the belief that there are no expected results in the face of performed efforts. As a result, they give up when there are new challenges and unfortunately make no effort.

On the other hand, optimists treat failure as a temporary indisposition or "lack of skills", which is not something that will last forever. Thanks to this, when they are defeated it helps them to become better players.

How does the event explain style work in practice?

When we encounter difficulties, we respond by thinking about them.
Beliefs quickly form our thoughts, which in turn becomes an automatic response - a pattern of behavior in similar situations.
This is how the diagram looks like:

The negative emotions that you experience after failures are not directly related to the difficulties you face in reality, but **to your previous beliefs about these difficulties.** By changing the patterns of your thinking, you will change the way you perceive reality and become more effective at solving your problems.

How to do it?

1. See the connection between difficulty, conviction, and effect.
Every time you have negative thoughts or you feel bad emotions, ask yourself: "What caused this kind of reaction?". Arouse your own curiosity and observe. You will quickly find out that there are certain situations in which you automatically react. Some negative reactions are completely unconscious, and you regret others after a while.

2. Write down how this scheme works in your everyday life
Write on a piece of paper 5 situations from your own life, according to the difficulty - conviction - effect scheme.

DIFFICULTY

Start with a situation that caused destructive emotion. It does not have to be a situation related to sport – think about any situation.
It is important that it is relevant from your point of view.

Examples of a football player, Robert:

- *"My parents asked me if I started to think about my future plans "*
- *"I lost at the end of the match"*
- *"My coach yelled at me during the training"*

CONVICTION

Write down what thoughts appeared in your head as a result of the situation. How did you interpret them?

Examples of a football player, Robert:
- *"My parents don't believe in me. I don't know what to think anymore... "*
- *"I never manage to bear the pressure"*
- *"I think I am useless and I can't be good at anything"*

EFFECT

Write down all the emotions that you felt at that moment. How did you feel after the whole event?

Examples of a football player, Robert:
- *"I felt depressed and insecure"*
- *"I felt completely powerless and discouraged"*
- *"I felt anger and hatred towards my couch"*

You will very easily see, that this kind of conversation leads almost every time to discouragement, passivity, and self-pity.

3. Change beliefs about the encountered difficulties.

Change your beliefs regarding the encountered difficulties and you will notice that your reactions to them will change. I recommend you 2 ways to deal with pessimistic thoughts:

METHOD 1:

Distraction - use it when you need a quick "help" for example during a football match.

- Say it out loud or in your mind **"this is enough!"**, *"STOP"*
- Imagine a **very loud bell** or a big **red STOP sign**
- Imagine a departing elevator with thoughts, turning a page in a book with a negative thought.
- Wear a rubber band on your wrist (it can be with a motivating quote) that you can look at or pull at any time
- Replace the negative thought with a keyword, e.g. *"Pull your chest forward and fight!"*, 'You do it for your dreams, so bring it onnn' etc.
- Reserve some time for such thoughts, e.g. *"Stop, I will think about it after the sports competition"*

METHOD 2:

Questioning - use *"calmly"*, at home, take a piece of paper and a pen.

Most of the negative beliefs are in our heads for so long that we take them for granted. We can easily distance ourselves from other people's opinions about ourselves (Think about how you will react when someone calls you an idiot) but we think that beliefs about ourselves are beyond any dispute. Most of your negative thought patterns are outdated, false, or borrowed from other people.

Questioning beliefs is all about looking for arguments against them. For this purpose, we can use these 4 methods:

METHOD 1: Proof

Having a pessimistic style of explanation, we act in a selectively, noting only the negative sides of a given reaction. Most often we exaggerate and catastrophize. If you did the previous exercises and wrote down your own negative beliefs, it's time to ask yourself:

> *"What specific situations indicate that I think so? "*
> *"What specific situations indicate that I am wrong?"*

Example:
"I can never stand the pressure!"

Evidence:
"Yes, I could not stand the pressure in the last match, but there were matches this season when I was doing quite well. You can't say I can never stand the pressure because the facts are different. "

METHOD 2: Alternatives
Once you acquire certain beliefs can be permanent like a so-called flea on a hound dog. Please note that each situation is different, and the final result may not necessarily be related to the lack of your abilities. Think about this:
"Are there other possible causes of unfavorable events?"

Example:
"I can never stand the pressure"

Alternatives:
"I felt like I was under a lot of pressure, but it was a very important match. Perhaps if I trained more often, I would feel completely confident and won this match. I will train well next month and see if it brings any effect"

METHOD 3: Implications

Sometimes belief that you have is true. In such a situation you shouldn't panic. It would be much better to think about what should be done to change this situation. Your weak link is reflected in your weakness only when you don't do anything to change or improve it. Think about this:
"If my belief is true, what can I do to improve the field to which it relates?"

Example:
"I can never stand the pressure"

Implications:
"It's true. Once again, I lost because of overwhelming stress. It cannot happen again because I can't show my full potential. From next week, I will start practicing meditation 15 minutes a day. "

METHOD 4: Suitability

When negative thoughts start attacking you during a competition, ask yourself about the usefulness of this belief at this particular moment. If you decide that right now it does not bring anything good, distract that thought using techniques that you learned in the DIVERSION section, and promise to yourself to rethink everything after the competition. Ask yourself this question:

"Will it help in any way that I'm thinking about it right now?"

Example:
"I can never stand the pressure"

Usefulness:
"STOP. It's not the right time to think about it. We'll talk tonight. Now concentrate, pull your chest forward and fight! "

For the next week, you should listen to your inner voice and question what appears in your head. You will notice how many beliefs are outdated or false. Try to write everything down, including the positive effects of training.

The techniques you've learned are not a magic cure for all your problems. However, if you get familiar with them, it will mean that you have the choice of how to feel about them. It is not the difficulties that are your problem, but the way.

"I just hate losing and that gives you an extra determination to work harder."
Wayne Rooney

17. ENTER THE FLOW STATE

*"I once cried because I had no shoes to play soccer, but one day,
I met a man who had no feet."*
Zinedine Zidane

The state of flow, called "flow" is a wonderful experience of being completely immersed in the activity. This feeling takes your per-formance to a completely different level, and when you experience it, you present 100% of your skills. Time is no longer important, and you have complete control over the course of events.

To experience the flow, you need to **match challenges with skills** so that your goal is ambitious but realistic.
Take care of the difficulty of the task.

Don't bite more than you can chew, or you'll get discouraged.
Don't set tour tasks too easy, or you'll get bored.
Pay attention to the chart below and think about what kind of task can make you find yourself in the flow channel. Often our flow escapes because we concentrate too much on ourselves instead of the task. We analyze how we fall out in the eyes of others, what impressions we make, wonder if the trainer will be satisfied, etc.

The key to flow is to **focus on the here and now**. Your mental energy is limited. If you start using it to think about your mistakes (past) or the consequences of failure (future) you will have little of it left.
You have to tell yourself: relax.

You must be able to see everything that
is going on around you, your sense of observation will become more acute, you cannot achieve this state unless you relax.

> *"I always want more. Whether it's a goal, or winning a game,*
> *I'm never satisfied."*
> *Lionel Messi*

18. CREATE A SUPPORTIVE ENVIRONMENT

"I have the chance to do for a living what I like the most in life, and that's playing football. I can make people happy and enjoy myself at the same time."
Ronaldo

I am sure you are familiar with the expression "Who keeps company with the wolves will learn to howl". It is very pertinent. Humans are a social being. We influence others, and others influence us. The worst thing that can happen to us is if we live in a bad environment, and we do not realize it.

In one of the interviews with Robert Lewandowski, he talked about how he consciously resigned from Saturday partying with his colleagues, because he wanted to be in good shape on Sunday. Was he on the sidelines of his environment because of this? Certainly not. In my opinion, he gained huge respect in his group.

As the years go by, we start to understand that **chasing for the acceptance of others is really the first step to mediocrity.** If you keep doing the same things as others, you can expect similar results.

Our best Polish player understood very early in his life that he is in charge of their own destiny. The dedication of your free time to the realization of your blurry dream appears very often in the biographies of outstanding athletes.

Surround yourself with people wiser than you, so will aim to be equal with their level. Surround yourself with ambitious people and you will be able to support yourself in your endeavors.

Surround yourself with positive people so that you see everywhere the opportunity to grow, not to complain.

> *"Before kids can play like a pro, they must enjoy playing the game like a kid."*
> *Steve Locker*

19. TRAIN WITH PEOPLE THAT ARE BETTER THAN YOU

"Believe you can and you're halfway there."
Theodore Roosevelt

Many athletes fall into this trap, which is the lack of development due to setting your goals too low. They reach a certain level that at a given stage of development becomes sufficient to cope freely, such as playing in the game in a 3-league team, after which they remain at this level for all their lives. This level is very often described as a comfort zone.

Falling into the comfort zone is one of the biggest nightmares for athletes. It is the time when you become a strong point in your team, people praise you and you are recognized by the local supporters. Your ego is feeling amazing. You become addicted to such emotions, and you realize that if you decide to move to a better club or league you will have to try all over again. In such a situation uncertainty occurs.

Your skills always develop in accordance with the difficulty of the chosen task. If your teammates and opponents are weaker than you, then you don't get the right training stimulation. Why would you even try to be faster, more precise, stronger, etc.?

When you are training with people that are better than yourself, you immediately try to be as good as them. You are being more focused on training. You give 100% of yourself because it's the only way to win a place in the team. You start to observe, imitate and train things that you didn't know that you can improve.

You train more than ever before. And by that, you get better and bet-ter. After some time, you again reach the point where you will have to choose:
To feel comfortable or uncertain?

> *"Success is most often achieved by those who don't know that failure is inevitable."*
> *Coco Chanel*

20. REJECT THE TALENT MYTH

"I am thankful for all of those who said NO to me. It's because of them I'm doing it myself."
Albert Einstein

Studies made by Kevin Anders Ericsson, the famous researcher in the field of expert psychology proves that mastery in every field can be achieved thanks to 10000 hours of "intentional training" (approx. 2 hours a day for 14 years). Of course talent matters, but only at the beginning of your adventure with a field. Fromthe perspective of a person on a professional level, talent does not matter at all.

So, where did this so common talent myth come from? Probably because people have always **loved to admire superheroes who were born with the "divine spark."** It's always been more attractive this way. Therefore, we very often encounter situations, where we will rather say: *"Wow! He is a genius! "*, and not:
" *Wow! What determined hard-working person!"*

What is more, the myth of talent is perfect for justifying our failures in every single field.

"I did my best, but I don't have the talent to do it." – it is much safer for our brain, rather than saying "I have tried, but I just simply didn't put enough effort to accomplish this."
So, what things should be included in the previously mentioned "intentional training", so it can lead us to the final champions? Here is the answer:

1. It should develop your skills, not keep them at the same level.
2. It must be prepared so you can focus on each and every individual component
3. It should measure progress and get feedback
4. It should have an appropriate level of difficulty that will be challenging for you.
5. Must go beyond your comfort zone and should not have anything in common with pleasure
6. It must be performed in total concentration and with the intentionof doing the exercise as good as possible.
7. It must be performed with a lot of emotions.
8. Should be repeated until you obtain total control.

STORY OF KOBE BRYANT – told by his coach:

"I've been a professional trainer for over 16 years, and I had this opportunity to work with many players. Some of them were on a high school level, others on professional. Currently, I am training with Bengals players (Cincinnati Bengals, NFL) .
After observing a few slam dunks made by Kobe in recent few matches, I decided to describe a situation that happened a year ago. I was invited to Las Vegas in order to help the US team prepare for the summer London Olympics. As you may know, they were supposed to win gold. In the past, I had this great opportunity to train Carmelo Anthony and Dwyan Wad, but this was my first time working with Bryant. We met three days before the first exhibition game, on the first training day which was at the beginning of July. We talked for a moment about his training, exercises. I asked him what goals he wants to achieve before the season and how everyone wants to win a gold medal. Then we exchanged numbers, and I mentioned that if he needed additional training sessions, he can contact me anytime. On the eve just before the first match, I was laying in the hotel room watching Casablanca, it was 3.30 in the morning. I was almost asleep.

Suddenly, the phone rang – it was Kobe. I answered the call.
- Hi Rob, I hope I'm not disturbing you? – Errr, no. What's up, Kobe?
- I was thinking, maybe you could help me with my training?
I looked at my watch, it was 4:15 in the morning.
- Sure, no problem. See you in the training hall in a moment.
I was ready within 20 minutes. When got to the training hall, I saw Kobe. He was all wet ... and sweaty as if he had just come out of the swimming pool. It was almost 5 AM We trained a bit for the next hour and 15 minutes. Then we went to the gym, we did some strengthening exercises. It lasted for about 45 minutes. Then I got back to the hotel, and Kobe was still practicing on the pitch. I felt exhausted and went to bed, and the next day 11 AM I had to be in the sports hall.
Of course, when I got up, I was feeling very sleepy - thanks a lot Kobe! I quickly ate a bread roll and went to training.
I remember the next part very precisely. All players from the USA team were on the basketball court, everyone feeling relaxed before the first match. LeBron was talking to Melo, Coach K was explaining something to Durant. On the right side of the room, I saw Kobe throwing the ball. Our conversation looked like this: I approached him, patted his shoulder and said:
- You did a great job this morning. - Hm? - You know, this training that we had in the morning. You did a great job. - Oh, yes. Thanks, Rob. I really appreciate that. - When did you finish training? - What do you mean? – You know… practicing throwing the ball. What time did you leave the training hall? - I'm just about to finish. I wanted to shoot over 800 throws, so now I am almost done. I felt like struck by lighting. Mother of mercy. It was at that moment when I realized why he had played such a good performance last season. Every story about his diligence, sacrifice, every quote about hard work. At that very moment, I recalled everything. Therefore, don't feel surprised that he is much better than players 10 years younger than him, and previously he had the highest average points per match in the NBA."

Talent, predisposition, ability to learn very fast will never guarantee your success. At most, it may help, but the quantity and quality of your training are fundamental and crucial.

In order to fulfill your sports dreams, you need to develop a strong ethic of work and train much harder than the competition. There are no exceptions to this rule.

> *"I always did something I was a little not ready to do. I think that's how you grow. When there's that moment of Wow, I'm not really sure I can do this, and you push through those moments, that's when you have a breakthrough."* Marissa Mayer

21. TRUST IN YOURSELF

*"Don't judge each day by the harvest you reap but by
the seeds that you plant."*
Robert Louis Stevenson

The basic fundamental of being effective in any situation is faith in your own skills and abilities. When you face a failure, you start to doubt yourself, it's hard for full commitment. A large proportion of athletes have a problem with this. Before they are defeated by the opponent, they lose by themselves.

Confidence is based on the belief that **no matter what happens to you, you'll find a way out of this situation with a defensive hand.** This attitude teaches patience.

There is nothing worse for an athlete than a fatal sense of letting go, mental surrender when the match is still going on. You can lose, but always after the fight to the end. This is characteristic of great masters.

Be your best friend and adviser. One who always believes in you and motivates you when you fail. **When negative thoughts begin to form in your head, try to look at yourself from the side and think about what your best friend would tell you. Prepare yourself keywords that will change your mindset and give you strength.**

*"The question isn't who is going to let me; it's who
is going to stop me." Ayn Rand*

22. CREATE YOUR PRE-START ROUTINE

"You can't outwit fate by standing on the sidelines placing little side bets about the outcome of life. Either you wade in and risk everything you have to play the game or you don't play at all. And if you don't play you can't win."
Judith McNaught

When you reach a situation, where negative thoughts begin to form in your head, try to look at yourself from a different perspective and think about what would your best friend tell you. Prepare a list of keywords that will change your mindset and give you more strength.

A pre-start routine is a previously prepared, repetitive behavior before each training and competition. Having a meal at the same time, putting the required equipment to your match bag, a specific time to reach the competition place, a similar warm-up, etc. Routine brings order to consciousness. The brain then works according to the learned pattern and as a result, we save our mental energy.

When everything goes right, just the way you planned it before the competition, you will start to have a greater sense of control over the whole situation.

Such routine will take your mind away from your stress and it will allow you to fully concentrate on the forthcoming task.

What should I do?
1. Think about your own sequence of thoughts and behaviors that will help you enter the state of full concentration.
2. Find the right music that will put you in the right mood.
3. Create an action scene in the event of unforeseen circumstances.

"Always go with your passions. Never ask yourself if it's realistic or not."
Deepak Chopra

23. DON'T LISTEN TO HATERS

> *„Don't take personally what others say about you. Especially when instead of helping you - they do everything to discourage. The only person that knows what you can achieve is you, nobody else! Take the words of others just as feedback, but never take them personally."*
> Michael Jordan

Every success works like a magnet that attracts haters. What they do is by diminishing your achievements they want to fill their own failures. Unfortunately, negative reviews from anonymous people can create unnecessary confusion in your head.

It is not a good idea to read online forums where haters spread their unhappiness. Human jealousy is a common phenomenon and it is not possible to change it. Words and reviews of frustrated fans are one of those elements of playing sports that are totally beyond your control (see Method 7).

Do not read reviews about yourself, and certainly do not enter into the discussion.

If you need a reliable assessment of your attitude, ask your trainer, teammate or your loved ones.

> *"Life is inherently risky. There is only one big risk you should avoid at all costs, and that is the risk of doing nothing."*
> Denis Waitley

24. START TO LOVE STRESS

*"Saying it is impossible to live without failing at something
is impossible. Unless you live so cautiously that you might
as well not have lived at all, in which case you have failed by default."*
J.K. Rowling

Stress is an integral part of human emotions. Nature has given us this feeling so we can survive. It was a way of notifying against the impending threat. And today things haven't changed, but unfortunately too often it paralyzes in the face of challenges.

It is impossible to completely eliminate stress from our lives. However, we can significantly control it, and it can even work in our favor.

A low and controlled level of stress - the one that does not cause negative reactions in our body, has a very positive stimulating effect and it can prepare players for an important event.

In a dangerous situation, our physiology changes. The heart beats fast-er than usual and the breath becomes fast and shallow. Inexperienced athletes often enter the competition in this way.

Analyzing for many hours and thinking about what will happen, reconstructing black scenario, focusing on your stress - it leads to one thing: failure. Trying to eliminate stress makes it even worse.

There is an old belief that what we run away from always gets in excess.

Face and accept your fears. It's part of you, me and every human being on this planet.

Tell him, that you understand why he is there and thanks that he reminds you of an important event. Many athletes like mild stress before competitions, so-called "adrenaline". Such stimulation is a strong stimulus for action.

> *"Don't worry about failures, worry about the chances you miss when you don't even try."*
> *Jack Canfield*

25. PRACTICE SELECTIVE ATTENTION

"If you are not willing to risk the unusual, you will have to settle for the ordinary."
Jim Rohn

Think – Isn't it worth liking this mild version of such emotion. Call it different. From now on, it is not "STRESS", but "small stress". When it appears – put a smile on your face and invite for cooperation.
During the competition, a lot of external factors are fighting for your attention. Most of them cannot be manipulated because they happen without your control. It is only up to you which signals will reach your consciousness. If you "invite" them to your mind, they can stay there much longer than expected, transforming into negative thoughts, emotions, and behaviors.

Remember that your attention has its limits. Being focused on many phenomena that are happening at the same time, will drastically reduce your efficiency. There is no chance that so desired by athletes muscular automatism will happen.

The effective concentration is based on selective focusing on the most important (from the player's point of view) signals coming from the environment. For example, the volleyball player who focuses only on the service ignores whistles coming from the stands, conversation under the player's net, previous actions, etc.

Studies show that professionals present a greater skill of selective attention than amateurs. They know why they are on the pitch, what they must do "here and right now" and what to do in the event of a temporary failure.

Analyze your previous performances for distractions (distractors) that have managed to distract you. Divide it into internal (such as your thoughts and feelings) and external distractions.

The most common are:

INTERNAL:

- Worrying about mistakes made in the past
- Thinking about what happens if I win, lose. What will happen if I fail my team and other things that are about to come
- "Choking" under pressure. Excessive muscle tension
- Excessive performance analysis (checking skills)
- Exhaustion. Negative internal dialogue
- Inappropriate motivation. Thinking about things that are completely not related to their performance.

EXTERNAL:

- Visual (audience, scoreboard, fans)
- Noise during the competition, music, fans, etc.
- Attempts to distract opponents e.g. offending, foul play.

When such threats to your concentration occur, you can use the following ways:
- A few deep breaths: Inhale the air for 4 seconds – Hold your breath for 2 seconds – Exhale the air for 4 seconds – and for 2 seconds don't breath
- Keywords that will remind you about the concentration in this very right moment, e.g. 'Focus', 'Just Do Your Work' etc.
- Keywords that will motivate, e.g. 'Fight for every ball', 'Pull your chest forward and have a constant confidence' etc.

- Visualization of a perfect performance
- Thinking about tactical assumptions, game strategy
- Your own playlist with your favorite music that will put your mind in full concentration.

> *"Success is a lousy teacher. It seduces smart people into thinking they can't lose."*
> *Bill Gates*

26. TRAIN MORE OFTEN THAN OTHERS

"Strategy of Coach Bob's is very simple. It consists of the words: make a habit of doing things that others don't feel like doing. For example, if others decide to take a day off on Sunday, it would mean that we can be one-seventh better."
Michael Phelps

You must know that training four times a week for 2 hours will not make you a famous world-class champion. The best players in the world like Ronaldo, Messi or Lewandowski train for 4-6 hours every day in order to reach the TOP class level.

If you decide to fight for the highest sports goals, your workouts must be on a world-class level. Check for the information on how to train individually. Start to use your creativity in order to prepare exercises on the pitch and don't fool yourself that you need a colleague to train.

With such an attitude you will live in the constant belief that you can't train yourself. By such action, you will never achieve success.
I have some tips for you regarding training yourself. But I must warn you – they are not easy. You have to demand a lot from yourself and you have to be totally focused.

Analyze your strengths and weaknesses:

Write down on a piece of paper your top 3 skills, e.g. Shots from the outside of penalty line, free kicks and receiving the ball from an angle. Now write what is your weakest point, e.g. playing with your head, dribbling and receiving the ball from the air. Once you've listed your strengths and weaknesses, first focus on your weaknesses.

You can train using a high wall to improve your head and to receive a ball from the air. Look for a place where you will be able to bounce the ball, for example, a wall or a board and train these elements each day for e.g. 50 repetitions. You will immediately see how your skills suddenly increase, especially your confidence.

You will no longer be afraid to receive a ball flying from the above or to hide your head when you have the ball to shoot. You can train dribbling by investing in a few bollards and kicking the ball with variable speed, different parts of the foot.

What is more, after defeating a few bollards, you can improve your descent on your right or left leg and shooting after a long or short pole. Don't forget about your strengths. Remember that you also need to practice them every day in order not to fall out of practice.

Here is an example exercise of dribbling with shooting:

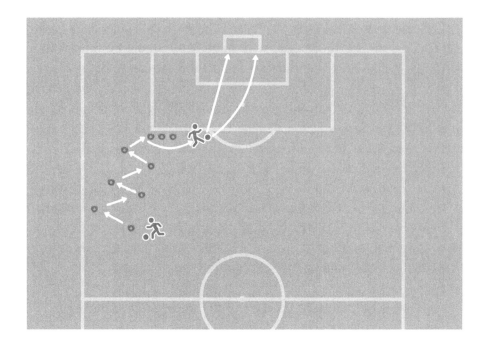

Prepare and write down your workout:

If you don't have a plan for your training, that would mean it is already weak. The fundamental for the increase in your skills is conscious train-ing. Write down 4-6 exercises, describe them precisely and carry them out.

Go the field with a ready plan (be prepared what you will be practicing). You will be more focused on exercises, and you will also save your valuable time on arranging effective training. You always need to have in mind why you are going to the field and for what purpose.

Turn off your phone and other electronic devices:

Remember that in the training there should be only you and the ball. When you are fully focused on your previously planned exercises, you'll get the most out of your workout. Also, you will get closer to your dream goal.

Turn off the phone and other electronic devices and make sure there are no other distractions. Spend 1,5 - 2 hours on training being alone and you'll see how your skills will increase day by day. Concentration is one of the main keys to achieving success in sport.

"I am currently training to play with my left leg, accelerating and shooting free kicks. Lately, I have not been good in these areas, but I know I will improve. "
Cristiano Ronaldo

27. DO NOT FORGET ABOUT MOTOR TRAINING

"Before the training, he always appeared first. The training was beginning at 11, he checked into the club at around quarter past nine. He went to the gym, did his exercises. Next, he went to the masseurs, just before he started training with his team for an hour and a half. After that, he got back to the gym to stretch a little longer "[Jerzy Dudek]. "He came first and finished last." When he was a teenager, "he thought that he is definitely too slim, so he lifted weights and ran for 40 minutes on a treadmill. (...) He was able to wake up in the middle of the night and sneak out into the gym. He did it two or three times a week. " According to Jorge Valdano, a former football player, "he works hard no matter the circumstances. One day he receives the Golden Ball, and the next morning he goes training. (...) When he wins the match, the next day he goes to training. If he doesn't win, he does the very same thing – goes to training. " Jerzy Dudek on Cristiano Ronaldo

Many athletes that are playing in the lower leagues think, that the gym will slow them down, and they will not be that fast. That's nonsense. It is an excuse against additional training. Motor preparation is the fundamental of faster running, pawning on the pitch and avoiding injury. Find the right person with good knowledge that will train your strength and running skills for the TOP level.

You will see how you will feel after the first month. Your body will adapt to heavier load on training. You will be able to train more, better, faster and harder. Injuries will not occur when your tendons strengthen, your muscles increase, you'll be a complete football player, an outstanding athlete.

After 90 minutes of playing, you will still be thirsty for physical exercises, even if you gave 200% of yourself. Scouts will see you. They will look at you with disbelief, that such a prepared person like YOU plays at such a low level.

Your testosterone will increase. What would that mean? More **SELF CONFIDENCE**, which you will use in various situations, for example when you play with a much stronger rival than yourself. You won't be afraid of running a duel or to have a close contact. When your opponent stands face to face with you, they will be scared. You will be in the winning position.

Look at Ronaldo or Lewandowski. How would you feel now if you stood face to face with them? You look at them and know that these are very serious players. You cross out at the very beginning and you haven't even started to fight with them. Perfect your running technique, train strength and you will see how much benefit it brings. And if you do not have money to hire a person who will prepare you properly, you can always learn by yourself.

Go to YouTube, look for that knowledge, there are hundreds of channels from which you can learn. The only thing that limits you is your mind.

> *"Many of life's failures are people who did not realize how close they were to success when they gave up."*
> *Thomas A. Edison*

28. BE IN CHARGE OF WHAT YOU EAT

"If you don't do what's best for your body, you're the one who comes up on the short end."
Julius Erving

Once you start training more often, you will also need to get energy from somewhere else for such an effort.

Good food is a necessity. What you have on the plate depends mainly on how you will feel the next day and how much energy you will have. Your body will recover much faster, the injuries will decrease, your desire to train more and harder will increase. Your sleep quality will improve significantly, you will sleep less and more efficiently. Avoid monosaccharides and fast food on a daily basis.

Add to your diet Fresh fruit and vegetables. Your menu should be based on low-processed products. Remember to read the label on the products. The less chemistry in the food, the better for your body. Test on yourself different products, observe your body. Check which products affect you well and which products not.

Of course, you must keep your so-called "healthy head" so as not to get into a bad Nutrition habits. When you feel like eating chocolate or pizza from time to time, do not hesitate, feel free to order the largest pepperoni pizza and eat it with a smile. Of course, don't do that the day before important competitions.

Do it as a reward after the struggles on the pitch.
In this way, your head will be able to reset before the next hard week of achieving your goal.

> *"Those who dare to fail miserably can achieve greatly."*
> *John F. Kennedy*

29. ANALYZE YOUR GAME

"Twenty years from now you will be more disappointed by the things you didn't do than by the ones you did do. So throw off the bowlines. Sail away from the safe harbor. Catch the trade winds in your sails. Explore. Dream. Discover."
Mark Twain

Always analyze your game. What does it mean in practice? Let me explain it to you. I have two verified methods, that work best for me.

The first method relates to **RECORDING MATCHES STREAMED** on the television and later watching at least one or two players playing in the same position as you. This is the fundamental of improving your game. Let's suppose that you are playing on the position of a striker and Bayern is playing against Borussia. You record that match.

Later, make a cup of tea, relax, sit down
with a notebook and a pen and while watching, focus only
on the movement of the striker from the Bayern team. Observe how he runs, how he creates free space, how he gets out of a difficult situation under the pressure of two rivals. When you focus and watch one player you suddenly start to learn at an incredibly fast pace.

Over time, you will play the ball by heart and each pass will be accurate. You will know how to move in a particular situation.
With such an analysis, you open your mind on the pitch. You start to perceive the match differently and situations that were once terribly hard for you, suddenly become very easy to solve.

You shall notice how this player is observing the whole pitch and his opponents. Stop the match, analyze how the player is making his choices. Even if he makes a mistake and misses the ball - you are in the phase of learning. You have to analyze both the good and bad choices. Do it consistently every evening and you will see how your movement on the pitch and the choices you make the change.

The second method is to **ANALYZE YOUR OWN GAME.** If you have such an opportunity, ask one of your closest friends to go to your match, so he can record it. After the match, you can easily look at the recorded material. You will be able to see from a third-party perspective how you move, what choices you make, what needs to be improved, and what to focus on.

Also, pay attention to your emotions, whether you are angry when you ruin the simplest pass or when you immediately run to pick up the ball. These are the details that decide whether you will play on the best pitches and fight for the Champions League or you will stay at the level of an unaware athlete in a league that no one has ever heard of.

> *"Whenever I climb I am followed by a dog called 'Ego'."*
> *Friedrich Nietzsche*

30. REGENERATE YOUR BODY AND MIND

"I knew that neither my coach nor probably Ricky will approve it, but we have reached an agreement on my needs so that I can function effectively as an athlete. Over time, I learned to understand not only my body but also my mind. After I got back from Beijing, I found out that sometimes I need to leave the house and have fun with my friends, dancing and partying. For me, it was a kind of "safety valve", which helps me with excessive pressure caused by life in the spotlight. Those moments with friends helped me with my training and no one, I repeat, no one could take it away from me."
Usain Bolt

All the points that are mentioned in this book are very important, but for me, the most important point is the last one which relates to the regeneration of mind and body. When you are in constant pursuit of your dreams, training at maximum speed, you can easily forget about good recovery. I have several proven methods, where you will quickly recover after a few training sessions. Try to put them in practice and you will see how your skills begin to increase even fast-er when you are fresh and ready for hard work the very next day.

Go for a swim: It is an amazing form of resting and in the same way to train mentally and work on your endurance.
Being in the swimming pool you will focus on every movement of your hand, you will clear your head and you will be able to calmly analyze your match/training (depends on your needs). What is more, your muscles will calm down after a hard day of training and it will give them the incredible slack which is required to reach the top. Also, your sleep quality will drastically improve.

Use the roller: After each workout, use the auto-massage (if you have one). Use it in the form of a roller or other massaging device. Roll each and every muscle very carefully and slowly so that your tired muscles pump blood much better.
What is the benefit of that? Faster and more effective regeneration.

Go to a physiotherapist: Let a specialist take care of your body. He will know how to relax your muscles. You will be able to see how it is done and what your tired body is facing. This way you will protect yourself from unwanted injuries and your awareness regarding training will dramatically increase.

Stretch: A very forgettable form of regeneration used by footballers. When your effort is increased, stretching your muscles has to be an integral part. Such muscles will be more flexible, which will result in better endurance and thus it will prevent various muscle from breaking and strains.

Meet with your friends: We have to be honest that you can't stand long thinking only about football or other sports. Your head will need a stepping stone from constant motivation and pursuit of reaching your goals. If you feel that you are burning out or that you don't want to train, or even that your workouts are not fully committed, take a day or two days off. Go out, meet with your friends, go watch a movie in the cinema, etc. After such a day, your desire and motivation for training will come back again with even doubled strength.

> *"Flaming enthusiasm, backed up by horse sense and persistence, is the quality that most frequently makes for success."*
> *Dale Carnegie*

SUMMARY

When you read all the tips that are mentioned in this book and put them into practice, you'll see how your sports career will significantly change. You will be an athlete who is conscious with a specific goal in mind and you will strive at all costs to make it come true. Remember that it is dependent only on your inner will, whether you want to achieve it or give it up at the start. Get ready for a real fight with yourself. When you will not feel like training or you start to train when someone tells you that you are weak and you can't do it.
You will not care about those opinions, you will just do your work and strive each and every day till you reach your designated goal. Slowly and systematically implement your new beliefs in everyday life, observe closely yourself when you want to let go or you don't give your full 100% potential. Believe in yourself and your skills.
If you're going to try, go all the way. Otherwise, you shouldn't even start. It can mean that you will lose your girlfriend, friends,
but remember.... **GO ALL THE WAY.**

As Mahatma Gandhi said, *"First they ignore you, then they laugh at you, then they fight you, then you win."* You will not know how to face with success or failure if you don't try to do your best.
Go, train, be active, win and remember, you only have one life.

JUST DO IT!

Printed in France by Amazon
Brétigny-sur-Orge, FR